In Search of the Wholey Sale

Birth of a Salesman

by

Cory Steiner

Dedicated to all who constantly strive to the highest levels and never give up no matter what.

Table of Contents

Birth of a Salesman

Understanding the true nature of the sales profession is a journey that doesn't happen overnight. People often look at the success of others and simply don't see what it took to get there. I had one employee who copied literally every aspect of my business model, except for one, and lasted for 2 months. There was one critical element that was missing.

There are no shortcuts to what we all seek. The goal is to do it the right way for the long-term and be a beacon of professionalism for which others turn to when in need.

"In Search of the Wholey Sale" will present that journey with multiple short essays into the mind of the professional.

I'm particularly proud of the essential components presented in the chapter titled "Sell Like a Marine" because I learned these qualities from some of the finest people that I will ever know. They were taught to me simply by following the example from those oozing with character, integrity and competence and, in looking back, I'm stunned to have been so lucky.

These critical qualities seem to be very elusive out there today, but this is precisely why so many are placing an ever increasing value on them. Be that shining light and you can literally do no wrong.

Customers are more intelligent now than ever which will, in effect, decrease your competition. They tend to treat all salespeople as guilty until proven innocent, but will soon recognize you as someone with whom to partner with in helping to make the best decisions possible.

The Intro to "In Search of the Wholey Sale" is titled "Birth of a Salesman". That could take on many meanings, but for me I view that as my entrance into Part II of my career. The challenges never end and, in fact, are intensifying in today's climate, but I feel so good about where I am and how I got here that I'm compelled to share.

Introduction

One of the earliest memories of my sales career was reading an article about a gentleman celebrating his 20,000th sales call. I was struck by that number and kept track of my own tally right from the start. I stopped counting several years ago somewhere in the 18,000's and am now well beyond the arbitrary target of 20,000.

I was new to sales upon leaving the Marine Corps having been placed in a top company by a fabulous recruiter specializing with Junior Military Officers. To say that he pointed me in the right direction is the understatement of the century. It didn't take long for the idea of a very unique book on sales to pop into my head.

The goal of this project is to present the principles of outstanding and long-term sales. I will demonstrate how the skills, leadership traits and values internalized as a Marine Corps Officer were the foundation of the effort that has brought us together to this point.

I waited until now to initiate this guide of excellence because I strongly felt the need to build the credibility through my own career to earn the right to proceed. They say that overnight success takes 20 years. In my case it was closer to 22, but having arrived during the worst time that my industry has ever seen is all the encouragement I needed.

Sales is the exact opposite of what many think it is and those who understand its most basic concepts can expect a lifetime of extraordinary success. The success we will discuss comes in the form of long-term relationships and a true consultative professionalism that your customers will rely on for the duration.

You will help others to achieve their goals while achieving your own with the most important leadership trait as your guiding force - putting the needs of others before your own.

It's not going to be easy; nor should it. In fact, it would be much tougher if easy since everyone would be doing it. If you stick with me you'll find that persistent people begin their success right where everyone else ends in failure. Both groups endure the same exact challenges and obstacles, but one moves on to a higher level and one doesn't.

Thank you for joining me in the Introduction as I now turn to writing the first chapter, "Confessions of a Sales Rep".

Confessions of a Sales Rep

There are 3 general categories of sales reps - Employees, Distributors and Independent Representatives. Employees are salaried with benefits, expenses, etc. Distributors buy products for resale and may also have employees. Independents represent one or more companies and receive commission-only on what is sold in their defined territory.

I began my career as an employee of a major pharmaceutical company selling chemistry analyzers to hospital labs and physicians' offices. Looking back, I'm stunned at how easy it was. I had 45 customers who I relentlessly presented new offerings to and ended up Rookie of the Year Runner-Up, #4 in the nation and #1 in my region on all measures of sales performance with what now seems like minimal effort.

A serious hip injury while racing motorcycles led to an immediate interest in orthopaedics which, in turn, led to my entrance into becoming an Independent Orthopaedic Sales Rep. It was very exciting until trying to schedule my first appointment. "Huh" was often followed by a dial tone.

Have you ever had that sinking feeling that you've just made a horrifically tragic error? Fortunately, some significant success was only 6 months away, but I clearly traded a lot of security for independence.

Some say that the greatest security is in taking the risk, but it's also often true that the grass isn't always greener on the other side. It is, however, greenest where most watered.

Sales According to Cory

Sales according to me is irrelevant. Everyone has their own unique style, goals and environment. What works for me might not work for another, but customers do tend to consistently respond to universal themes.

My early and continued success is a direct result of putting myself in my customers' shoes and determining my approach with a high level of empathy. How would I like to be sold to in this setting?

All fingers pointed to the low-key approach where I give customers all the information that they need to make the best decisions for themselves. This not only makes selling a lot easier and more enjoyable, but also more professional and positions you more as a consultant and less as a typical sales rep.

Sales According to Cory is simple (and will often be repeated throughout this discussion) - put your customers first and yourself last. That is the magic formula that will put you on top and keep you there.

Fortunately It's Difficult

Sales in and of itself is easy. The difficulty is in making sure that you're offering what people want in a way that they can seamlessly get it.

There are so many variables and obstacles today, many of which are out of your control.

The niches that made me rich and famous (sports medicine orthopaedic devices) actually disappeared about 17 years into my career (for a variety of reasons). I did everything I could to save a market that didn't exist anymore as if a Japanese soldier lost in the jungle after the war was over.

The next step after finally admitting defeat was a thorough reinvention. I couldn't just offer a superior product anymore that would solve a common problem - I had to also bring significantly more value into a physicians' practice to keep up with the ever-changing times.

After much error & error I was able to identify the best way to accomplish these new goals. You must, today, bring more value to your customers than ever before. You must constantly be aware of rapidly evolving market conditions and do your best to stay one step ahead.

You have to eat, sleep and breathe your career not only for your own survival, but to bring new ways to those you serve to ensure their survival as well.

And regardless of how tough it gets you must remain long-term focused and never compromise your integrity for anyone under any circumstances. If your gut screams "red flag" it's a red flag and you are to pass on that opportunity or destroy the reputation you've worked so hard to develop.

Sell 'til You Drop

Certainly, one of the goals is to work smarter; not necessarily harder, but one does have to pay one's dues. I'm up to 1 million or so miles shuttling between sales and cold calls. It would seem as though much of that was wasted time, but it was identifying where to go and where to not go so that I may work, well, smarter.

There really is no substitute for hard work. Putting in those long hours is "The Secret".

Also, I suggest "Sell 'til You Drop" as a reminder that you're not selling when you're not in front of a customer.

I have a friend whose success is in the upper stratosphere of what we all seek and he continues to blaze new trails. He is constantly looking for new opportunities and new ways of serving others. His charitable contributions are equally staggering as a sterling example of the "cycle of life" in sales - helping others to achieve their goals leading to achieving your own which then provides the resources to help others in other capacities.

Helping others truly has no limits and is the core foundation of selling and the source of joy for anyone in its path.

Sales Managers - Guilty Until Proven Innocent

I am extremely fortunate to have had my very first sales manager as my most important mentor. He was a classic "corporate" sales manager who had a thorough understanding of all of my customers and provided me with the information that I required to serve them to the best of my ability. We were both relentless together in our pursuit of always putting the best interests of others before our own and I take great pride in how our shared values created a team approach that served everyone well.

Some of my other sales managers along the way weren't quite so integrity-riddled. A good sales manager is more of a teammate and less of a boss.

I had one humdinger who was with me while presenting a very nice shoulder brace to an occupational therapist. She first unsuccessfully tried to apply it over her medical jacket. While taking her jacket off to get a better fit he blurted out in a horrific attempt at humor, "You might as well take your shirt off too."

She angrily said, "Excuse me!" as I was repeating "NO" several times while slowly stepping back. I must have blacked out because I don't remember anything that happened after that, but ultimately responded by banning him from ever setting foot in my territory with me.

I lost that product line soon thereafter, but chose to part gracefully rather than fight that battle.

I've since learned that having a bad sales manager just isn't worth the hassle. Good companies know how to conduct themselves so seeking employment with the reputable should resolve any of these issues.

The point is to never under any circumstances compromise your integrity for any reason. Another point is to embrace the knowledge that most sales managers wish to share and make them an important part of your team.

Sales people whether in the corporate or independent world prefer freedom and independence, but don't overlook what we can learn from one another.

Something's Gotta Stick

My Independent Rep career began with an entire wall of phone books representing every square inch of my territory. I identified the target audience and then wrote down every single name and address. Several worn out maps later helped to identify where the opportunity was and where it wasn't.

The amount of work it took to get to that point was staggering and never-ending. There's simply no easy way and I always get a kick out of those who seek similar success, but burn out after 2 months when reality has sunk in.

A typical evolution is to go absolutely everywhere all the time making each cold call count with the goal of getting the appointment. It's a numbers game, but don't seek numbers for the sake of numbers. Try to make each cold call count even if only demonstrating to the receptionist that you're a pleasant person. That'll make your next visit potentially more productive.

Something has to stick and it will. Just blaze a trail, don't stop and try to improve daily. The number of relationships developed will increase in direct correlation to the effort expended.

I've found that good things always tend to happen when at an emotional low point that I just push through. Maybe it's just some sort of universal law of nature since it seems to happen every time and those low points are just part of the cycle.

So get out there, don't overlook the value of being depressed and always have a smile on your face no matter what. And, certainly, cold calling should remain an important part of your strategy for your entire career. There's something refreshing about it.

I Am Not an Animal

One of my favorite encounters is when approaching a receptionist (or other office personnel) with my usual thoughtfulness and goodwill only to be greeted as if having 2 heads. It's hard to explain my response since it just comes naturally, but it's kind of a jovial acknowledgement of rudeness. It's almost like a nice icebreaker.

There's nothing like being charming to office staff who are in misery for no reason of your doing. They'll typically remain frightening, but there's an outside chance that they'll subconsciously like you after you're gone and realize that they were a jerk for no apparent reason.

The goal is to develop relationships. The actual prospect may have even witnessed your behavior from around a corner and might take the time to review and consider your offering.

The point is to never take anything personally even if it is personal. Everyone has challenges and sometimes a little compassion goes a long way.

I had one very good customer in my first position after leaving the Marine Corps who was so difficult that even my sales manager said that she's not worth the effort. I thought that she was cold and heartless with no soul, but was told that she frequently asked about me after I left.

You never know for sure how you're going to be perceived or what sort of positive influence you might actually have on someone who's never before been given the time of day.

How Much for That Bridge

Someone once said, "I'd rather be the person who bought the Brooklyn Bridge than the one who sold it." That didn't immediately resonate, but its meaning didn't take long to grasp.

Given the choice would you rather be trusting and naïve or void of character and integrity?

The answer is obvious, but it's still important to note those who bring dishonor to our noble profession. Is it really worth the short term gain? Do we really want to try to fool others or would we rather take pride in being a professional consultant who always has others' best interests in mind?

Our number one quality that prospects ultimately seek is trust. We have to maintain that 100% of the time especially when no one is watching. When it's all over you will very much appreciate reflecting back knowing that you did it the right way. Those you serve deserve that, you deserve that and that's what you want.

Stay true to character and integrity and, although it will take time, your name will consistently come up when others seek professional guidance in your industry.

Trust me.

I'd be Nothing Without the Competition

Times have changed tremendously particularly over the past 6 or 7 years. Selling used to be fairly easy, but it's now hard and I think I know why.

My early competition and I had a healthy connection. We liked and respected each other and fed off of one another. I remember, early on, leaving a meeting with my most successful competitor in my rear view mirror. We were and are still very friendly, but I said to myself, "I'm going to get you" as I sped away. We've both achieved the success that we seek for which I'm grateful and glad for him as well.

For many reasons (in most if not all industries) opportunities have dramatically changed. The challenge is to not only find where those new opportunities are, but to also create them - to bring even greater value to your customers than ever before since their environment has similarly evolved.

This is hard, difficult work not for the faint of heart. Failures are typically greater than successes in this brave new world that we're all navigating, but all too many are seeking the easy way. There is no easy way. Those days are over.

On one hand, maintaining good values today helps us to rise to the top. On the other hand when professional peers sink to new lows it lowers us all and we have to somehow go the extra mile over time to prove to our prospects that we're to be trusted in this new environment of greater disappointment around every corner.

Similarly, we all benefit when our industries are inhabited by professionals of impeccable character. We all rise together to the top serving others to the best of our ability. We learn from one another and continually find new ways of being extraordinary.

Born to Serve

I arrived at college in the summer of 1981 as a typical 17 year old with limited direction and clarity, but had the good fortune of observing many who were the exact opposite. There were qualities that I noticed among the ultra-successful. Many seemed to share and demonstrate a rare level of humility, intelligence and integrity in all areas of their lives in this culture of ethics that I strived to be a part of.

Seeking military service was my way of ensuring continuity of this endeavor. I knew nothing about the military, but the Marine Corps seemed to fit the bill to the T. Had no clue what I was getting myself into and would have made the decision sooner if I had.

It all became clear halfway through Officer Candidates' School. My peers were dropping like flies with an eventual graduation rate of 40%.

The culmination was a desire to serve; specifically, how to help others to do their very best at all times. In sales that correlates to "How do I provide my customers with the best information that they will need to make the very best decisions for themselves?"

I believe that we're all born to serve others to the best of our ability. We just have to be introduced to the mutual gratification that comes from service and it then just becomes natural.

Sell Like a Marine

The impetus of "In Search of the Wholey Sale" was to present the entire scope of selling and how it's founded on the highest levels of character, integrity and good morals and not strictly on an empty transaction void of substance.

With that, I'd like to lay out the fine points of leadership as I was taught and observed as a United States Marine. These traits are nothing new, but are what it's all about. Make them your own, live them every day all day and everything you touch will turn to gold.

Set the Example

Keep Your Word

Courage - Stand Up for What's Right (even if you're the only one doing it)

Be on Time

Get the Job Done Without Being Told

Be Friendly and Respectful

Treat Everyone Equally

Be Enthusiastic and Let Others Do what They Do Best

Be Neat and Clean

Share Unpleasant Tasks

Put the Needs of Others Before Your Own

Privately Correct Others When They're Wrong

Help Someone Who's In Trouble

Judgement - Weigh the Facts

I'm Good Enough, Smart Enough and People Like Me

Professional sales can, at times, wreak havoc on one's self-esteem. Whether in the corporate world or on your own there's a level of self-motivation required that most have trouble sustaining.

The backdrop is the sheer number of "no's" that you hear on a daily basis. This number is often a consistent percentage of effort expended. It may take 50 "no's" for a single "yes". Naturally, one can then conclude that it takes 100 negative responses for 2 positives. But, with the proper work-ethic you can live quite well on your 2% success rate.

Of course, you will become smarter with experience so your 2% success rate could gravitate towards 5% or even more. You just can't, though, get around putting in the time with the corresponding blood, sweat and tears.

Don't, however, confuse a "no" with an actual "no". Oftentimes it's a cry for more information. "No" just means "Not now".

This is consistent with putting the needs of others first. Don't make it about you. Help others understand by giving them all of the information that they need to make their own best decisions. Go at their pace. Follow their lead on how to best proceed and watch your success rate increase.

The foundation of having the confidence to endure is that you always, without fail, conduct yourself with the very highest levels of character and integrity at all times; especially when no one is watching. You always let the best interests of others be your guide so you will never have any reason to be self-conscious. You have the ability to look a prospect right in the eye and not blink. You have earned the right to approach them with your offering and they are waiting for you to do so.

This is the quiet confidence that will eventually, if not already, make you not only a leader in your industry, but very possibly THE leader. Some things never change and this is one of them. Market conditions, politics, perceptions, etc. are in a constant state of flux, but trust never goes out of style.

People do like you because you're among the few. It may take longer for you to make the sale, but once you make it you'll keep making it and constantly evolve in whatever way is required to serve others to the best of your ability.

The Art of Selling Without Selling

My entrance into orthopaedic sales was supposed to just be an entrance. It readily became clear that I missed the positives of the corporate world and almost immediately set out to identify the #1 company in the industry. I asked several surgeons and all responded with the same name.

After relentless correspondence with the local and regional managers I found myself pulling up for the first interview. It was with the regional manager and all was well until he asked me what my favorite sales technique was. I had been building my own little business for exactly 1 year with some significant successes and that question stopped me dead in my tracks.

After a few seconds of panic it occurred to me that I use no sales techniques at all. My approach is founded on providing my customers and prospects with all of the information that they need to help make the decisions that will be best for them. I can honestly say that I only once directed a customer to make a decision that was best for me and that lapse in judgement still haunts (even though the customer never knew and still doesn't and I did get the sale).

Interviews 2 through 4 were with the local distributor of orthopaedic implants and devices - a legend in the industry. We had many common interests and really hit it off. I was excited beyond belief. This is what I wanted with every fiber of my being; so I thought.

Then, right before being offered the position some things happened that highlighted the enormous effort expended over the past year building my business. I won't bore you with details, but I was now in the most dazed state of confusion humanly possible. I knew that an offer was imminent so some serious soul-searching had to be done quickly.

I was simply unable to make a decision so my gut told me to not give up on what I had built. A call to my new friend followed with me profusely thanking him for his time and explaining why I just can't jump ship.

He graciously understood and appreciated the gesture even before being offered the position (out of respect to him and his associates). But, more than anything, that experience helped me to clarify what would follow for the next 24 years - being a different type of sales rep. One who prides himself in good products, good support and being a consultative resource founded in trust, mutual respect and real solutions.

Integrity is the Bottom Line

We often speak of the bottom line, but how do we get there and is the traditional bottom line really the bottom line? Sometimes we focus too much on the ball and lose sight of what it takes to get it over the goal line. It's really more about the journey and less about the end result because the desired result doesn't happen without the proper journey.

The concept of integrity didn't become internalized until several weeks into Marine Corps Officer Candidate School. We had a difficult physical exercise with many different stations that you'd progress through only after completing the task at hand.

Although difficult, the instructions were simple. Complete one task before moving onto the next and none of us knew that we were being watched like a hawk. 2 of my peers moved onto the next task without entirely completing the current one. Both were gone the next day never to be seen or heard from again.

I actually witnessed both infractions and they seemed at the time to be extremely minor. I thought nothing of it and was, naturally, shocked of the severe action against them. But, they didn't do what was asked of them. It was really like a shock-wave infusion of the qualities absolutely required of a Marine Corps Officer at all times without compromise ever for any reason.

The theme of integrity is the common thread that we all shared for the remaining time spent on Active Duty (and beyond). Once you experience real integrity in all manner of conduct it's typically ingrained for life. You understand its value and importance and just can't shake it. It's why you'll often hear, "Once a Marine Always a Marine."

When we apply this to sales, family, education, etc. the sky isn't even a limit. One certainly need not have served in the military to embrace these values - many do. I'm just making the suggestion to be aware of integrity and the other principles of leadership previously discussed because this awareness and internalization of these values will enrich your life and those of others beyond your wildest imagination.

When the going gets tough there's one thing that no one can ever take away from you. You guessed it - your integrity. It's more valuable than any sale that you'll ever make.

Integrity, in fact, is the bottom line.

The Infantry of Business

I remember my months of initial sales training at the corporate headquarters of a major pharmaceutical company and marveling at the scientists, engineers and medical personnel that we'd frequently happen into. I felt rather inadequate at times surrounded by so many profoundly intelligent and well-educated leaders in their field, but it didn't take long to discover that nothing happens without us presenting their masterpieces to the world.

We are The Infantry of Business in the trenches completing the cycle that culminates in putting their ingenuity (in this case chemistry analyzers and instrumentation) into the hands of the end-user.

We learned very early on as a Marine Corps Officer that no one is any more or less important than anyone else. Everyone performs a very important function that, as a team, completes the mission. No rank, duty or assignment reign supreme. We're all in it together with the mutual respect and admiration that are critical to achieving our shared goals.

On one hand it's a bit ambitious to put myself in the same category as a PhD scientist, but we all do have our own unique aptitude and skills. And if we were to swap jobs for a day we might find that everyone is best served by swapping back as quickly as possible.

Road Joy

With well over 1 million miles logged I've developed a few Rules of the Road that promote fun and safety. Fortunately I'm a huge fan of driving and do most of my own repairs. Regular oil changes are of utmost importance as is all scheduled maintenance and constantly checking tire pressure. My current car has 246,000 miles on it so far and I'm shooting for 500,000+.

But, the single most important rule by far is to never engage in any type of road rage regardless of circumstance. I'm eternally happy-go-lucky, but have still been on the receiving end a handful of times from no fault of my own.

Recently I was driving exactly the speed limit with a red light in sight and a driver on my bumper looking very upset trying to get to the stop light as quickly as possible. As I slowed to a stop he pulled next to me in the shoulder screaming bloody murder.

I feared that he had mere seconds to live so I gently unbuckled my seatbelt, took a slow deep breath and he illegally sped away in the shoulder. Maybe the calm approach frightened him away, but my heart rate didn't go up a single beat and I was having coffee at Dunkin Donuts within minutes. No harm done.

I've come to the conclusion that someone who's stupid will remain so regardless of my response so it's probably best to not respond. I've seen all manner of dangerous driving, texting while driving, running red lights, driving off the road into a pole and the aftermath of accidents. I say a prayer every time I start my car and keep a few sentimental items within view.

I find the road to generally be a joy, embrace it and look forward to driving to my next appointment or cold-calling excursion. I try to avoid rush hour traffic patterns and gravitate towards scenic routes if not too far out of the way.

The road is one of your most important tools so use it wisely and safely and may we all have another million miles.

They're in a Meeting

Possibly my single most favorite phenomena is when calling customer service and told that no one is available because they're in a meeting about customer service. I live for these moments. It is my favorite thing.

After a few decades of this I've accumulated scientific evidence that one is either born with a working concept of customer service or one is not. This cannot be learned. You either have it or you don't and I can identify a person's ability in this crucial area within 5 seconds of speaking with them on the phone.

I've worked with very experienced customer service personnel that are worthless (or worse) and been introduced to brand new employees that are utterly fantastic and a true joy to work with for many years.

One tell-tale sign of pending doom is placing an order while driving and having the customer service rep asking me for the customer number. It's not possible to know a customer number while driving so I explain that and it never sinks in. They persist upon every order called in as I resist driving into a truck.

The good news is that more than half of the population is capable of outstanding customer service. It is our job, then, as professionals to either try to get the failures replaced before they do too much damage or to inform our customers of these challenges that we'll have to periodically navigate.

One of the companies that I represent as an independent rep constantly hires extremely ineffective customer service representatives. They've also had some tremendous national sales managers who didn't last long. I've come to accept them for who they are, don't get to wrapped up in it and pretty much do the minimum to get by while minimizing any difficulties that they frequently cause customers. They have a great product and a profoundly disconnected CEO and there are certain battles that just aren't worth the effort.

Embrace your friends in customer service that are outstanding because they are worth their weight in gold if not more.

I've Fallen and am Getting Up

Not to harp on the negative, but it can be very difficult out there today. Market conditions and environments are constantly evolving and in a very erratic state of flux. Customers face the same challenges of uncertainty while they attempt to do more with less as we all try to navigate through to the next level. Some are struggling just to maintain with the corresponding high stress levels that can make our jobs seem impossible at times.

There are times when we lose a critical sale, lose an entire product line or may even find ourselves out of work. We can be the best at what we do one day and then out of a job the next.

I'm often asked how to get into medical sales today and usually respond with "you don't". If they ask again then maybe they have a shot.

If you can accept that you'll be frequently beaten down one way or another then you are ready to embrace the negatives and use each as a stepping stone to the next positive. Each failure is a learning experience of what not to do or what to do next.

Failure, then, is your friend. It's not the goal, but an essential part of the journey to the greater heights that you'll never reach without being injured (sometimes severely) along the way.

People often view difficulty as a bad thing, but it is a great thing for many reasons. Anything worth achieving will be difficult. Not sure why, but it's just one of those laws of nature that's consistently true. Also, competition thins as difficulties and challenges intensify. Each piece of the pie often gets larger as the overall size decreases - another fundamental law of nature that we may sometimes overlook.

I'm one of the last of the old-time reps in my industry. Some have moved on to "more secure" jobs, retired, died or worse, but the new faces tend to not last long. A career in sales is not for the faint of heart (especially today), but it's probably the best time for the few and the proud.

Trust is gained over time. There's no other way so if your face is the one that remains then you are the one who will keep increasing your business while the rest make excuses outside of themselves for their own failures.

No matter what happens to you take a deep breath as you lay in the mud, shake it off, regroup and develop a strategy that's never before been seen. Keep trying new things until something works with the ultimate goal of offering the best to your customers and prospects with a relentless smile and goodwill.

And yet another law of nature that for some reason is always true when I'm at my very worst is that "When the Going Gets Tough Many Doors Open".

"Commission" and other Four Letter Words

I guess that even I have preconceived notions of salesperson stereotypes that I go to great lengths to dispel. Maybe it's from getting brutally ripped off at a car dealership with my first purchase - a used 1985 Toyota Corolla. A great car that served me impeccably well, but I questioned what had just happened when the salesman walked away pumping his fist.

For some reason the word "product" sends me into a tailspin. It seems to depersonalize what we're trying to present as just another product void of anything unique or valuable. Anything can be a product, but we don't offer just anything.

Other words evoke similar feelings of dis-ease. Words such as sales, selling, sold, commission and so on. "Present" is a much better alternative as is "fee for service" if it ever comes up.

We are professionals and have to use professional language and correspondence.

Anything that puts the focus on us and our benefit must be avoided. It's all about the benefit to the customer or prospect. We meet their needs first which is then how our needs get met. Our success is a byproduct of putting the needs of others first.

We are not trying to close a sale - we are opening a relationship. Use words consistent with building a relationship. This is how we differentiate ourselves as the leaders in our field.

We listen twice as much as we speak (consistent with having been given 2 ears and 1 mouth). We don't want to concentrate so much on making a living that we forget our true calling of making a life. We've chosen the profession of sales to enhance the lives of others and then, consequently, enhance our own.

This is who we are and it all starts with the accurate perception of us by those who we wish to serve.

It Was a Good Death

Sometimes you just have to let it go and move on. Whether a customer that's insane, a company that just doesn't fit or a disaster that you have to recover from you will have to periodically assess, evaluate and adjust. The only thing that's permanent is change.

Those who never make mistakes simply miss opportunities to learn. Some even suggest that success is 99% failure. Probably better to minimize that number, but the point is a valid one. Maybe a better way to say it is that nothing really ever goes wrong.

Letting something go, whether by choice or otherwise, is often painful, but can initiate some very significant seeds of inner drive. Our past challenges, really, are essential to becoming who we are today so why stop now. Sometimes you literally have to jump off of the cliff and build your wings on the way down; hopefully in time.

When we are defeated we are, in effect, urged to greater effort. Defeat is a gift that makes us grow. It's like a grindstone that can either grind you down or polish you up. You consciously decide whether to harden your will to achieve or your will to complain and become depressed.

It all goes back to your attitude. A great attitude equates to great results with a poor attitude leading to poor results. You get the exact result that you expect. I've always believed in myself through the worst challenges of my industry (which haven't yet gone away) even though sometimes I'm the only one. No one defines me but me. No one else has my permission.

My most difficult decision was made 8 years ago when forced into shifting focus away from my core group of customers who I spent my entire career developing amazing and remarkably satisfying personal relationships with to a somewhat unknown that many beat me to by 25 years or more.

The business that I cultivated, to make a long story short, didn't exist anymore so I had to change. It was sad, difficult and very rocky. Many things were tried, mistakes made and discouraging partnerships came and went, but I got there.

My business didn't change, but its theme did. The easy days are over, but I've honed myself into a leader in this new frontier using the same exact moral code that led to my previous success. Fortunately I wasn't smart enough to know to move on entirely maybe back to the corporate world or something more stable, but sometimes the greatest security comes from taking the risk.

Ultimately, though, the only one who can cheat you is yourself. Trust your instincts - your mistakes might as well be your own and not those of others.

Take This Lunch and Shove It

The debate on whether or not to provide lunches to office personnel rages on. I've done maybe a hundred or more and most have netted nothing. As a medical sales rep I used to do frequent lunches at all of the orthopaedic resident training programs in my territory all of which netted exactly nothing.

Let us, however, not throw lunches completely out of the window. Sometimes they are very worthwhile, but you have to be the judge and prequalify. A suggestion is to first ask if the prospect might actually be interested in your offering. That's not by any means a guarantee, but can be a viable start.

I would definitely advocate lunches, etc. for good customers as a showing of appreciation, but sales reps serving as a catering service is much more often abused than not.

Once I was providing lunch for 8 residents and was running late so I confirmed the number and asked if they could just order and I'll pay upon arrival. Soon after my entrance a team of pizza delivery people marched in with a corresponding drop of my jaw.

They had ordered pizza for the entire medical college and, as luck would have it, there was an ATM machine right there. I went moderately insane for a brief period and did no more lunches for several years.

A few years ago I made a triumphant return to providing lunches and then remembered why I stopped doing them. Most of the time nothing good comes from it unless you enjoy wasting time and money and getting annoyed for no apparent reason.

With qualifying lunches comes qualifying customers. If it's a good risk then I'll do it. If it isn't or if I'm not sure then I won't. If it's a good customer who I'd like to reward then I will.

The efforts to abuse the sales rep in this regard continue and my usual response is that we have a No Lunches policy for now that may or may not change in the future. If I'm in a bad mood I might say that my goal is to bring enough revenue into your practice where you'll be able to finally be able to afford your own lunches.

OK, so I'm a little bitter about this, but the fact remains that it's usually a terrible idea that will get you nowhere. You'll know when it's a good idea and, in those cases, you'll serve everyone best by rolling out the red carpet and sparing no expense. But most of the time you'll serve best by sparing yourself the expense.

If you disagree with me you're not necessarily wrong (and I'm not necessarily always right), but that's my opinion wrought from years of abuse and I'm sticking with it.

Real Marines Have Dirty Boots

I remember once while on active duty conducting a live fire exercise at Camp Pendleton, CA and having a senior officer from another unit stop by to observe. He approached and introduced himself, but was taken aback by me not saluting.

For several reasons, one being safety, we generally didn't salute while in the field firing live ammunition. I tried to explain this and went from bad to worse. Most peers and seniors were fantastic, but this one was a bit inflexible.

He reported me to my own chain of command who told me that I would have made life a little easier on everyone if I had chosen to not fight that battle and just saluted. All would have been fine and no harm done. Point well taken and I vowed to do better next time.

Additionally, we were out in the field getting dirty so I had made the conscious decision to not shine my boots that particular morning at 4AM before leaving home (or the night before). I had never seen this Officer before so maybe he was more used to a non-tactical environment, but he also suggested that I polish my boots next time. Not sure how I responded so I probably didn't say anything.

It was I, however, who was now taken aback. It didn't make a whole lot of sense to spend valuable time cleaning and polishing boots that were about to get over-run with dirt; time much better spent maybe getting a little extra sleep or studying up on the next day's exercises.

The vast majority (about 95+% from my observations) completely got it, but looking the part and being the part weren't necessarily one in the same. One doesn't just put on a Marine Corps uniform and automatically becomes a Marine. They have to go to great lengths to fill that uniform in.

Competence and results are far more important than how one looks although my boots were certainly spotless and properly shined when they had to be. And, to this day, I generally don't leave the house without properly polished business shoes.

The point is that anyone can look the part, but are you the real thing? Only you can decide and just asking the question suggests that you are. It's not who you are that can sometimes hold you back - it's who you think you're not. This is often inaccurate and you should give yourself more credit.

The only potential for ineffectiveness and underperformance comes from not being who you think you are which is often preemptively addressed through humility. Humble people, however, don't think less of themselves - they just think about themselves less and others more and it's what you learn after you know it all that really counts.

The Power of "Please" and "Thank You"

Good manners go a long way. Saying please and thank you at appropriate times, holding a door open for someone, waving a fellow motorist by when either of you could have the right of way, being respectful for the time challenges that others have, etc. all play a critical role in being a high-performing professional.

Sometimes the basics get lost or never make their way into someone's consciousness in the first place. Not that any of us needed it, but we had specific courses on this in Officer Candidates' School. Certainly didn't hurt and made sure that everyone was on the same sheet of music on these very basic concepts.

Even though very basic I do periodically get blown away by the behavior of professionals from time to time. A fellow sales rep joined me on a visit to meet with the #1 surgeon the nation specializing in a limb-lengthening procedure. This guy actually taught himself Russian specifically to convert the notes of the procedure's inventor into English. He was interested in our knee stretching device and couldn't have been nicer.

It was too late, but my peer was for some unknown reason chewing gum like a horse. In looking back, the appropriate response would have been for me to rip his throat out, but I just went with it and we did our thing. The physician did incorporate our device into his clinic so all was not lost, but it was a real head-shaker.

Another related potential deal-breaker is to do whatever is required to not eat like a pig in front of anyone. If your table manners during an interview process aren't impeccable you're not getting hired. I'll likely cut the interview short, pay the bill and throw your file into the trash on the way out.

So please don't overlook the power of good manners and the damage you create for yourself with bad form. Being aware of these details that some might view as irrelevant is just another part of the putting-others-first package.

You are the complete package and the last thing you want to do is undo all of your hard work with one simple oversight.

The Mission or the Marines

We had an ongoing debate while in our 6 months long second phase of training and were often split on our opinions. Was the mission more important than the Marines or were the Marines' well-being more important than the mission?

Some of us argued that the mission is more attainable if you put your people first. This will create an environment where they'll go to hell and back for you thereby greatly increasing the odds of completing the task at hand.

Others believed that nothing comes before completing the mission and that you simply have to figure out what's required for that to happen.

I got into a bit of trouble during our initial training (prior to this phase) where we had to complete an exercise that I was leading and one of my team members injured his knee. I completely disregarded the completion of the assignment in the specified time while we hobbled to our check point.

We obviously failed and the critique wasn't comfortable. I didn't complete the mission. I didn't even think it was important with the added challenge of a real injury, but I failed and that was clear.

What I should have done was to position my team member in a secure area where we could immediately retrieve him once we got the job done or quickly figure out a way to carry him along without causing more injury. Neither was even tried and I was personally made an example out of for what not to do.

The question still remains and it wasn't overly clear who won the debate, but it seemed like most felt that putting the best interests of your Marines above all else allowed you to accomplish anything and my experience beyond training confirmed that finding in a way that makes me a little emotional just thinking about it.

The theme of putting the needs of others above all else reigns supreme and it's proven over and over and over again. Why mess with success? Put others before yourself and everyone wins. Sorry for sounding like a broken record.

Marathon Training

I've run in 5 marathons over the past 7 years and wow is that a tough one. It's safe to say that the Olympic record remains safe, but one does learn about oneself by digging deep from miles 20 to 26+.

I began running 7 years ago and went right into the marathon. The better approach is to properly and gradually build over time. Rome wasn't built in a day nor was a marathon runner. My goal for now is to get more proficient at the shorter distances and then either revisit or stick with 5 and 10K's and an occasional half marathon.

In a very difficult environment, like today for many salespeople, you might find correlations to preparing for a marathon. It's truly a science project where one has to inch their way towards race day through proper preparation over time.

One might approach sales with some similar principles. Rather than trying to sell to everyone I hone in on the best targets and try to cultivate them through to completion and then provide whatever level of service and support that they prefer and require. Some customers are very self-sufficient and some aren't. Following-up with the self-sufficient ones, though, is still crucial so they don't forget about you.

Proper selling is more about the journey through the tunnel than the light at the end with some saying that there's just as much light inside. The process never ends nor does the learning as we continue to improve with no end in sight.

And when the going gets tough we try to maintain the steady pace that we practiced for about 700 miles of a typical training cycle. We will succeed not because of our will to win, but because of our will to properly prepare.

Wealthy Thinking Precedes Wealth

For some reason it's a lot easier to make money when we don't need it and seemingly much more difficult when desperately needed. Not sure why that is, but remains one of those pesky laws of nature.

The key, then, would be to pretend to be wealthy prior to actually accumulating wealth. I always say that I'm extremely wealthy, but that just the "money" part hasn't yet caught up.

Maybe the problem at times is that we lose focus on those things that money can't buy. We harp on what we don't have while comparing ourselves to others not realizing that we often already possess those things that those we envy long for that no one can ever take away.

It's quite possible that we already have acquired some serious wealth and that now with that as a solid foundation we can much more easily acquire the financial wealth that we seek. The hard work is done and we can now reap the rewards that are in direct correlation to the extent to which we serve.

This is the understanding that we must have before proceeding to the highest levels. We must maintain a perspective of what's truly important in our lives and in the lives of others and not allow ourselves to view achievement through a distorted prism of wealth without character. The more that we're grateful for what we have the more we will have to be grateful for.

One exercise that may be worth a shot is to view yourself at the end of your life having already achieved all of your goals and what it took for you to get there. Then do that. You will want to look back without a single regret and with the full knowledge that you did it the right way with honor, integrity and confidence. You left your mark and had a positive influence on many and will be remembered for who you are - not for how much money you have.

Wealthy thinking is priceless and comes at no charge.

The Gold Standard of Professionalism

Thank you very much for joining me in this journey to the highest levels of success in a profession that sets the bar high for those willing to accept the challenge. Be all you can be, do more before 9AM than others do all day and be among the few and the proud. A few good men and women are all it takes.

A clear understanding of the principles and traits presented and applying them in any area of your life will ensure maintenance of The Gold Standard of Professionalism that is so essential today.

You are capable of much more than you realize. It's behind a locked door in your mind accessible with the key of confidence that is within us all. If this eludes us then we must pretend to be confident until we become so. You've earned the right by desiring a life of honor.

Nothing is guaranteed as our only true direction can be found in constant change. We must continue to educate ourselves, find new ways and strategies and be ever aware of changing markets and customer needs.

Strategies for success are nothing new and no secret. The same principles that made people successful yesterday are the same that make people successful today (as well as tomorrow). A world-class foundation is in place and now the rest is up to you.

A Sacred Oath

At this point you get it. Maybe the next step is for me to learn from you. Certainly the next step is for others to learn from you. You have so much to offer and there's no better time than now. And I can't think of a better person since you are absolutely the best you that there is. There's simply nothing else like you anywhere in the entire universe.

I thank you so much for the opportunity to continue to lead by example. One of my greatest hopes is to have accurately presented who we are and how you can carry on the tradition. Almost nothing would please me more.

Another goal is to use this book as a guide for Veterans to demonstrate the value of the skills that they already possess and how to apply them to their next "duty station" in the civilian world.

Again, I thank you for the time you have taken with me and for your sincere desire to make your sales career one of the very highest levels of commitment to others. Leadership knows no boundary and the sales profession done right will allow you to help others to fulfill their wildest dreams while you fulfill all of yours.

Without further ado I offer the final 20 chapters of "In Search of the Wholey Sale" to fine-tune the strategies of uncompromising service.

Two Ears and One Mouth

There's a distinct reason why we were given 2 ears and 1 mouth. Real selling happens during the "listening" phase.

I was doing a recent presentation at a medical college in Philadelphia and, honestly, a little proud of how I commanded the room while speaking in front of a large group. Normally I'd be a little on the nervous side, but all the stars were in perfect alignment.

As I went on and on it occurred to me that I need to let others speak. It took some self-control, but some great discoveries were revealed as I transitioned from mouth to ears.

I didn't make a sale that day, but implemented a resource where I could sell to graduates once they left the college. Also, a new department was emerging that I'll be able to assist with once underway. Both of those opportunities appeared once I stopped speaking.

It's almost cliché to say, but a critical skill is to know when to shut up. How many opportunities are lost when we lose sight of the customer by remaining focused on ourselves?

Selling, just like leadership, is a 2-way street with neither party more or less important than the other. We each play a role of equal and mutual benefit to one another. We can't place too much importance on ourselves or too little on the customer.

It's an acquired skill, but using your mouth and ears in their intended ratio will help everyone to determine and reach their goals through the best solutions currently available. Sometimes it takes a lot of effort to identify that best solution, but made a lot easier by being pointed in the right direction by the customer.

Public speaking is great, but there's no substitute for public listening.

Partnerships Make the World Go Around

Sometimes, as sales reps, we get a little too caught up in our own independence and lose sight of how others can help us and vice-versa. I'll admit that oftentimes our professional peers may be lacking in certain areas, but much can be gained from partnering (one way or another) with those of like-mind.

As I approach my 25th year I'm somewhat in overdrive developing new partnerships. One is with a gentleman with a business model similar to mine who's introduced me to some new products that he benefits from when sold by me. I don't get my typical 100% of the earnings, but what I do get is a lot better than 0%.

Another is a former competitor who I've joined forces with to blaze new trails in this increasingly challenging environment. A lesser person would have some reservations, but the common ground is our shared goals and conduct so it's a no-brainer.

And yet another is forming literally as we speak. The interesting thing about this one is that it's in a niche of my industry that recently fell apart due to overwhelming abuse by many companies that took advantage of a lack of appropriate regulation (to make a short story shorter and to not bore you with details).

The dust settled and those who always conducted themselves honorably (a very small percentage) emerged back on the scene with the cream rising to the top seeking each other out. I was very honest with my concerns (almost to the point of being insulting) which revealed the exact same concerns he had of me.

The potential for creativity is endless, but care must be taken with who you associate with. I also have a few stories of partnerships that didn't go far so do approach with caution and be very selective. There are a lot of really great people out there just waiting for your excellence.

A Team of Mentors

It can get lonely out there, but made much less so by knowing that there's thousands (or more) of us also staring at our windshields on the way to the next appointment.

I had a little bit of early success and remember playing a profound role as a mentor to a new representative in the industry at my first large conference. It was the American Academy of Orthopaedic Surgeons Meeting in San Francisco where a new rep jumped right onto my coattails.

I guess I did a good job because he's now my mentor. A very successful leader in my industry I often call him for advice and he never disappoints. He's right 100% of the time which is probably why I call him so often.

There's others like him as well who I rely on for good advice when needed. I also greatly enjoy it when others call upon my insight and always do my very best to offer proper guidance.

I think that one of the best things that a sales manager can do is to connect the sales force even if just a simple list complete with territory and contact information. The value of periodic commiseration cannot be overlooked and is almost essential to high performance. We learn so much from each other to include knowing that we all have similar challenges. Just knowing that we're not alone, especially when it seems like we are, is of tremendous value.

And then, along the way, we develop various relationships that remain through thick and thin. My industry has really changed a lot with a sense that many of my peers from years past are gone. To my very pleasant surprise (at a national meeting held locally) some familiar faces emerged.

It's a real delight to have a growing list of friends as you continue to establish yourself in your chosen industry and periodically run into each other year after year after year. Your role as mentor and protégé are critical and appreciated more than you know.

It's the End of the World as We Know It and I Feel Fine

Positive thinking is one of your best tools to address anything; from minor disturbance to major calamity. There's a slight chance that I've been surrounded by negative thinking my entire life which is probably why I refer to several family members as Dr. Norman Vincent Peale whenever they're in not-so-rare form. Maybe my positive attitude is a form of rebellion. It has served me well regardless and I shall not relent.

For example, I used to race motorcycles and during a race at a major event near Pittsburgh I was in 3rd place on the last lap. Trying a risky maneuver didn't end well as I went over the bars, landed on my knee and drove my femur out the back.

There was an instant sensation I've never before experienced which indicated pending doom with the flagmen frantically waving the other competitors away from me as an additional clue. When the dust settled I asked the EMT's if there was any chance of just a bad sprain. They just looked at each other and said nothing.

Once at the ER the doctor (who was tremendous, by the way) said that we need to get right to work without medication because there was no time to wait for lab reports. He asked for my permission with my response of, "Well, it can't get much worse." Again, I was wrong, but it directly led to a great career in orthopaedic sales and marrying an orthopaedic nurse. How lucky can a guy get?

The point is that on one hand things often go wrong, but on the other hand nothing ever goes wrong. There's always a solution to every problem and quite often the solution brings you to a place that's even better than the starting point.

Honing in on another example was the reinvention of my own business after a very successful first 17 years. My business climate changed and I didn't. I had become complacent in a rapidly changing environment and didn't properly evolve.

The stars eventually aligned, but not after a lot of pain (which could have been minimized by being more proactive). During this time, though, I had total confidence even when I was the only one. I'm not saying that I knew the answers all along, but knew that I would find them.

And that's the key. When the world seems to be caving in with no end in sight it's your duty to carry on. Seek and ye shall find. Remain busy, blaze new trails and pick yourself up when one path leads nowhere. Oftentimes you'll find that there's many more paths right behind the next door; even if it seems to be permanently closed.

We often hear of young superstars that made it big early on yet, for some reason, we hear less of what really goes on out there. The truth is that many of the ultra-successful became that way in their 40's, 50's and even in their 60's. Way too many of us get discouraged way too easily not realizing that excellence is inside of us all and literally right around the corner. If not yet there you just need to keep pushing and it will come.

There was a time not too long ago when I absolutely did not have the answers, but kept at it and rebuilt my business one relationship at time. Before I knew it I was back and better than ever with no end in sight.

And it should be no surprise that what remained constant no matter what was the character and integrity that are the foundation of this book. Keep your eye on that ball and you'll go down a path where you'll never get lost.

You're the Best You There Is

Continuing with the theme of the previous chapter - when the going got tough fewer and fewer believed in me. I found myself trying to convince others that I was on the right track even if it didn't seem like it. I believed in me and, in looking back, that's all that really mattered.

Some family and friends meant well and were truly looking out for my best interests in recommending a career change, but there was no way I was giving up a successful career because of "a bump in the road".

Everyone today has unique challenges and very few just fall into great success. It's a bear out there, but misery loves company so all is well. Why, then, would one jump out of one frying pan into another? Thankfully, I made the conscious decision to remain in my current frying pan.

Business climates are changing now more rapidly than ever; or so it seems. Change, then, is a good thing and is where the opportunities lay (and this is nothing new).

Do not, I repeat, do not ever allow another to dictate the direction of your life; and that includes a spouse. Remain focused and true to the values that define success. And don't even let me define that for you. You define your own success and pursue that.

You were born an original and will serve others and yourself well by staying that way.

One exercise that works wonders is to create a vision of exactly where you'd like to be and then work backwards noting the steps, in reverse, that it took to get there. Not easy, but that's the point. The one factor that always jumps out is the enormous effort it took to reach your highest peak.

Not to sound like a broken record, but there's no shortcut to hard work and by committing to that you've just risen to the top. Actually getting there now is simply a formality.

Time Heals All Sales

They say it takes 5 visits to make a sale. I'm not sure who "they" are, but they probably haven't ever sold anything. It's more like 7+ with some sales initiated from years of repeated contact.

Regardless of what anyone says, patience is one of your greatest assets (assuming that you're a patient person). Unfortunately, some sales managers aren't patient and feel the need to pressure reps into behaving counterproductive to what is trying to be accomplished.

Some things cannot be rushed no matter how much you'd like to rush them.

In today's climate of volatility and uncertainty customers have already been burned by rash decisions and high-pressure tactics and are now very defensive; and rightfully so. It's your job, as previously mentioned, to be very patient and thorough in giving your customers and prospects all of the accurate information that they need to make the best decisions for themselves.

With leadership being the 2-way street that it is it's your job as a professional to work effectively with anyone above you who might be impatient and unrealistic. An excellent approach is to keep those who you report to very well informed.

It's easy to become a bit of an anti-authority, but everyone has their job to do and everyone wants to be successful. One of those critical times when your outstanding leadership is summoned is when those above you just don't get it. Part of your job, then, is to treat them also as a customer and do your best to ease their fears and concerns.

If they are truly an idiot (which is rare, but does happen from time to time) you are to remain focused, incredibly pleasant and do your best to minimize their influence without any fanfare. They will make extra work for you, but worse can happen and sometimes we step back when seeking the perfect arrangement rather than dealing with and rising above it.

So you see there can be many pressures, but you're not alone. Patience is essential, but so is striving to work well with everyone and taking the time to craft relationships with customers and everyone else who's part of your chain of command.

Time heals all sales by being one of its most critical elements. Never forget, as also mentioned before, that success often begins at the exact point where most others give up. Persisting isn't a natural response, but prospects also have a lot of pressures and concerns and will be ready to become one of your customers when they're ready; not when you tell them that they're ready.

The Strong Survive; or Those Who Don't Know Any Better

As we persistently beat the theme of "persistence" to death we conclude with what separates the best reps from the rest. I'll do my best to articulate what I'm trying to say. I first have to figure out what I'm trying to say, but you know what I'm saying.

I think what I'm trying to say is that sales today isn't easy, but the grass isn't always necessarily greener on the other side. We all have challenges and most of us are fairly average because we fail to overcome these obstacles.

Sales can be particularly frustrating because it's not a matter of punching a time clock and getting paid. It's a matter of creating value thereby making the lives of others better. We just have to figure out how to do that.

Still, though, greed and impatience seem to rule which, counterintuitively, halts progress dead in its tracks. More than half don't get it, but you do which is why you're still reading.

It all starts with a good product that your target audience can actually use. With the partial demise of my industry (caused by a series of factors beyond anyone's control) many in my shoes sought opportunities that were strictly about making money and not necessarily about serving others. Shockingly (or not so shockingly) every one of those opportunities was short-lived. Not only are those opportunities gone, but so are the vast majority of those reps.

When the going got tough the tough (like me) said, "I honestly don't know what to do." But, we remained true to the values of service to others and when the storm was weathered the few and the proud were the last men (and women) standing in a new brave world of remarkable opportunities. We had all earned the right to lead, consult and sell (both to customers and to the companies seeking our expertise).

Getting back to the title of this chapter, though, I think a smarter person would have left in search of greener pastures. If I had, let's say, an Ivy League Degree I'd be out, but probably making less money than I am right now even though the Ivy League graduate is much smarter than I. So, it can pay very well to not be overly bright. The last thing you want to do is to try to outsmart yourself.

Just stick to the basics with whatever you do and these are the qualities that will serve you well in any arena with an amazing force of attraction. I'm just thankful for how difficult it's been over the past several years because most of my competition is now gone.

Politics and Religion

It's common knowledge to not bring up politics or religion in sales, but we're not trying to be common here. We're trying to take charge, lead and be different in a very positive way.

Many problems today exist because people are adverse to having normal discussions and finding common ground. My-way-or-the-highway has replaced common decency and certainly common sense.

I was thinking of running for a state office in 2008 out of total disgust for the candidates on both sides who stepped forward. In typical fashion no candidate said or stood for anything. I didn't proceed because I'd rather do it right than jump in at the last minute, but one of my customers was thrilled and urged me to dive right in. She was so excited.

As our friendly conversation progressed it became clear that we were both on opposite sides of the political spectrum. I already had a clue, but have a preference to debate over preaching-to-the-choir. I'm actually rather soft-spoken and extremely friendly so she automatically thought that we were on the same side.

My goal during this tense exchange (and tense exchanges in general) is to establish the common ground that recognizes us as much more similar than different. We all too often get partitioned into groups that are expected to believe and behave in certain ways where we lose our identities and sense of self. We conform and cave to the pressures of the masses.

Isn't it better to have opinions and think independently while also respecting the opinions of others? This is how we learn, grow and improve.

After all, we're leaders and not followers. Our customers are intelligent with a greater chance of buying from you if they have a deep sense of your honesty. What better way to demonstrate honesty than by being honest?

In my view, then, having intelligent, reasonable and respectful discussions about politics will leave a lasting impression that no other sales rep will leave. You'll be remembered and appreciated.

I wasn't quite sure of the outcome with the customer discussed above, but when it was all said and done I think we both gained a perspective on some of the issues discussed that maybe neither of us had before considered. Of course, it was about health care and the final word was that we all pretty much seek the same thing; which is usually the case regardless of issue.

Not sure where religion comes in, but politics is a definite topic worthy of everyone's time.

A Finely Tuned Machine

Two areas of extreme importance that are often overlooked are the health of your vehicle and your body. I replaced my gas guzzler when prices hit $4.50 per gallon and my diesel VW Jetta with 246,000 miles and counting still looks and runs as if new. I do love my former BMW M3 and M5, but the simplicity of a reliable and economical car are far more valuable. And this has nothing to do with my hatred of BMW mechanics.

I am lucky, though, to live within walking distance of an incredible mechanic (who's honest and can do almost anything). A list remains at the top of my glove box with a complete maintenance schedule leaving no stone unturned; and then some. Whether I do a maintenance item myself or drop it off for completion this list remains a top priority. When due I typically do not pass go until done.

Cleanliness also reigns supreme with regular vacuuming, cleaning, waxing, etc. Time is always limited so I'll often do a little at a time on a never-ending cycle of upkeep. Remaining up-to-date with maintenance and cleanliness is a critical component of staying organized and a reflection of how you conduct yourself otherwise as well.

But the fine-tuned machine isn't complete unless its occupant is also properly maintained.

The importance of diet increases with age so, while on the road, I seek out salad bars and do my best to make healthy choices. Every now and then I have a complete breakdown at McDonald's, but it's OK to periodically fall off the wagon. My real weakness is Dunkin Donuts for which I'm trying hard to overcome.

Fitness need not be complicated. My recommendation is a nice and easy consistent effort of cardio, strength training and stretching. If you're like most, time can be very limited, but it's more than worth the effort to be healthy than to take the time to be sick.

The fitness options are endless, but the key is to be a student for life of fitness. Proper cardio, strength and stretching complete the package with constant long-term variety.

Personally, I like having a goal and really enjoy the "running" community. Everything about running is great except for the "running" part, but I try to not get hung up on details. I'm somewhat of an average runner, but am constantly improving.

Success with running cannot be achieved by running alone so I mix it up with different types of cardio, bodyweight strength training, weight lifting and stretching all designed to create a balance. The key, as with anything, is to keep it as simple as humanly possible (and that includes when training for a marathon).

Ask and Ye Shall Not Receive

Many a confidant will say to simply ask for the business and they do have a point, but let's not be premature. Have you earned the right to ask? Have you provided all of the information necessary to encourage others to make the decisions that are best for them?

If you're asking that question then the answer is probably yes because that implies that you get it. You understand that the key to everyone's success is in putting the needs of others before your own. Yes, I know this is yet another "broken record" alert, but one can't overstate this. You're either authentic or you're not and it's a very good sign if you're still here.

Your customers will perceive this and trust your judgement for they know that you're looking out for their best interests.

When the going gets tough most look for shortcuts and then, coincidentally, don't last very long. Both you and your customers are subject to similar challenges, really, so it's during these tough times that the most enduring relationships are forged. This also applies to those who you report to. We are all in it together and there is no doubt that we will all succeed together.

Ideally, your customer will ask you for the business, but you can certainly help them along. Now that you know without any shadow of a doubt that you are a leader In Search of the Wholey Sale you may ask for the sale without inhibition. Your customers know why you're there and are, obviously, part of your team.

The sale isn't just the sale. Some get so caught up in trying to make a living that they forget to make a life.

Get to know your customers beyond the sale. Look around to see what they're interested in. Family, peers, staff, etc. are all part of the complex puzzle you're piecing together.

Do it the right way, have no regrets and continue to grow beyond what you ever thought possible. The sky isn't even a limit so, what the heck, ask away. You've now earned the right. After all, one does miss 100% of the shots that they don't take.

You're Not Yet Ready

Kwai Chang Cain, in the 1970's TV show "Kung Fu", was told each week in the opening credits that he will not be ready to leave the temple until he can snatch the pebbles from his master's hand. A few frames of trying and failing culminating in a successful snatch signaled that it was now, in fact, time for him to leave. He had become a Shaolin Monk and, man, could he kick some ***.

As in writing this book, too, I had to wait for my credibility to surface before I could believably be a Shaolin Monk of sales. And it is not easy. A ton goes into getting to the point of readiness, competence and confidence (and I still have to occasionally remind myself to be confident and then it eventually returns).

My family and I drove through New Jersey to a party in New York City a few weeks ago and I reminisced about the thousands and thousands of miles wasted driving up and down that wretched Turnpike in search of business. But was any of that really a waste or part of the essential process to learn where the business was and where it wasn't?

In trying to answer that question for myself I think I can say that there actually was a ton of time and effort wasted, but was still necessary in learning how to work smarter and more efficiently. It's this frustration that signals a desire to get to the next level. Thankfully it's difficult. It not only thins out the competition, but also adds to the job security of those willing to go the extra mile or, in my case, the extra maybe 500,000 miles.

I often hear of stories of sales reps who are doing great and keep prospering with no end in sight. Nothing is more gratifying than hearing those stories. They give me a lot of hope when the chips are down and indicate that the opportunities out there are very real.

If you're like me and are in a tough industry you can blame no one but yourself. I'm right where I want to be even though there are probably other arenas where I may have made more money with less effort and drama. But this is who I am and what I do. It's what I know and what I enjoy so I just had to navigate through the rapids and keep repositioning into the right direction.

Many of you are likely in similar environments and the time comes when you come to realize that you're here to stay and love it no matter what. You've arrived and are wealthy beyond words even if the "money" part hasn't yet caught up. It will when you're ready and that day will arrive (if it hasn't already).

Am I Seeking Failure?

I think it was Einstein who said that the definition of insanity is doing the same thing over and over again and expecting a different result. Being insane, then, is a very common occurrence, but one to try to avoid if at all possible.

Can't say I'm completely innocent. We tend to get stuck in a routine or comfort zone that we resist venturing out from. It can be rough out there and embarking into the unknown makes it even more so.

We do, however, periodically get stuck in a rut with the natural tendency to sit at your computer and stare at the screen making excuses in an effort to avoid the discomfort of change.

One of my mentors said, very early on in my career, to start knocking on doors during these times. This, in fact, is the single most important time to do so with results that are entirely predictable.

Am I seeking more of the same or do I wish to blaze new trails?

It would be so much more difficult if it were easy. Every disaster and calamity creates a new opportunity to pursue. I sometimes view myself as a shark - yes, maybe I have a tiny brain, but I'm in constant motion and will not be defeated. I'm also like the Samurai where 2nd place doesn't even exist. Put another way - I will walk where failure fears to walk. I will work when failure seeks rest.

So what do I want and how do I get there? Do I remain negative and complacent or optimistic and energetic?

The time is now to get into good habits and to be keenly aware of your surroundings adjusting on a dime to ever-changing conditions and forces that are beyond your control. For every change in your industry is an opportunity to evolve into an area of greater prosperity for all.

Many of us, me included, get caught into the trap of blaming this, that or the other. It's possible that I've, in the past, blamed politics for the state of my medical sales industry and although that's true it does no one any good to not claim responsibility for my own outcomes.

These challenges and obstacles are nothing new and as old as the beginning of time. Looking throughout history you'll find a long list of the same exact complaints. Human nature doesn't change, but we can and doing so is the only way to rise to the very top and stay there. It's your sworn duty to do so and is the only option.

Luck Isn't Lucky

Since it often takes 5+ contacts with a prospect to get to the starting line and 50 or more "no's" for each "yes" you can see how much activity it takes before the sale is realized. The numbers can be daunting, but made less so simply by putting in the work. The only shortcuts that I'm aware of are hitting the lottery or receiving an inheritance; neither of which are an option.

I have a phenomenal new device that's rapidly become the foundation of my efforts, but doctors hearing "phenomenal" and "new" are 2 serious red flags.

My customer base with this new implantable medical device is growing very nicely, but it's truly been rough. Maybe that's why I'm so encouraged.

One practice, in particular, has 9 doctors and is my ideal candidate. I've lost count of how many times I've left information for the physicians and staff, but finally got a break to present it to them at 6:45AM a few weeks ago.

To make a long story short everything was perfect with the next step being a presentation the following week to all 9 doctors. That presentation never happened, but rather than give up I just made the assumption that I'll simply need another 30 contacts with the practice one way or another just to get me back to the starting point. No biggie.

I've been back 3 times since and got another big break. Upon approaching to leave additional new information for the doctor who spearheads new projects the head of the operating room was helping a patient to her car. I held the door open and stayed out of the way. Upon her return I offered a short summary while respecting her time and although nothing has yet happened I feel confident that I'm 1 step closer.

Most people at this point would have probably starting looking for a new job. Rather than sitting at home trying to figure out what to do I saddled up and happened into a very key staff member who's part of the decision process. I asked her if she could run this by the gate-keeping doctor and she said "yes" with a smile.

That wasn't luck, but the result of constant motion. Again, I'm not there yet, but am a little closer and will keep at it until the sale is closed and the customer supported, by me, with precision.

Part of this creation of luck is that with each contact you're reinforcing to the prospect that you're a professional that will be around to support them. You work hard, offer an excellent product and with each visit the natural defenses slowly drop until they're willing to give you legitimate consideration.

So, to be honest, I feel pretty lucky.

Freedom, Opportunity and Apathy

Someone once said, when asked about apathy - "I don't know and I don't care!"

I wonder if they're part of the 98% who, in a study that I've heard about, are incapable of being an unsupervised self-starting sales rep. Not sure if that number is true, but I'm also not sure that it's not. Of course there's more opportunity for the other 2% if that number is accurate.

We all have the same opportunity in this country regardless of what anyone says. It's literally endless, but is not easy so a huge percentage of us seek shortcuts that never pan out or just give up altogether. All too often we put in enormous effort to climb a seemingly insurmountable hill only to conk out just before cresting the ridge. It's very sad and I see it a lot; and often perpetrated by sales reps who are really great people.

With freedom comes responsibility. We are responsible to our families, to our customers, to the company or companies that we represent and to ourselves. And that responsibility can be utterly frightening because nothing is guaranteed. Sales can be a big risk, but the ultimate security is found in taking that risk. You'll often be a boxer in a tough 10-round fight, but your hand will be the one raised if you can remain focused, intense and honest with the person most difficult to be honest with - yourself.

I harp a lot on evolving (mostly because I didn't for quite some time). Whether you work for a large company in the corporate world, function as an independent sales rep, small business owner or the head of a household we all ultimately work for ourselves. We all have the same exact freedom to be enormously outstanding in everything that we do.

Those who fail are no different than those who succeed. They just take the path of excuses when the going gets tough and the tough take the other path that continues to climb up the mountain. Personally, I think it's easier to be successful than to constantly explain why you're not.

It's like a fitness program. You'll get stale and burn out if you continue to do the same exact workout day after day. You have to continue to change your routine. Evolve by learning new workouts, setting new goals and learning from others who have already accomplished what you wish to achieve.

I remember as a college athlete full of wishful thinking, but falling short on delivery. My goals weren't set high enough. I had one goal, achieved it and was content in being a loser. My excuse is that I was young and my brain just wasn't developed enough to get it. You do not have that excuse.

As we near the end of this book I command you to know who you are, where you came from and where you wish to go. See you there.

It Really is That Simple

For some reason I'm trying to improve my marathon performance with my annual participation in the Marine Corps Marathon. I improved my time by 20 minutes last month and feel like I could take another 20 minutes off next time by altering a few things and if it doesn't get to be over 80 degrees out like it did on October 30th.

I'm having second thoughts and might opt for the Marine Corps Marathon 10K instead. That would make a lot of sense, but my wife had to go and suggest that I not run another marathon. All someone has to do is tell my not to or that I can't do something and I just can't let it go. It might be from when I fell off my changing table as a baby. I'm really not sure.

But the point is that there's only one way to continually improve at anything. And that elusive strategy is to just get out there and do it. Those who are great at what they do have the same exact fears and concerns as everyone else. There's fundamentally very little difference.

We just believe and believe and believe and then act accordingly. I always say, too, that if you don't believe in yourself to just fake it until you do. It's only a matter of time and never gets easy, but that's a good thing. It makes us more exclusive and therefore more valuable.

I began running (for the sake of running) at age 45 and immediately became a student; certainly one that makes a lot of mistakes. My biggest mistake was spending considerable time in front of the computer trying to learn as much as I can about running. A very accomplished runner suggested that a great approach is to go out and run.

Selling is the same way. You have to get out there in front of people and keep blazing new trails and retracing old ones.

I purposely used that bad word, "selling", because it's now time to change the way people perceive the professional sales rep. We are valuable and a critical part of any team.

Other members of the team are also critical, but just fill a different capacity. On my team are physicians who consult with our companies and PhD scientists who develop the devices that significantly help real people. I cannot do their job and they cannot do mine.

They can be remarkable at what they do and out of business tomorrow. The same goes for me. I often say that the paranoid will survive and although optimistic, positive and highly motivated there's always that backdrop of paranoia that I'm not staying 1 step ahead of the curve.

One of the most common mistakes is that many of us are held back by who we think we're not (probably from the negative influences of others). Consider yourself right now as world class and then becoming so will come naturally. I swear to you it really is that simple.

Everyone Calm Down

As we navigate through the murky waters of striving to achieve greatness we will invariably be exposed to various members of our team who occasionally freak out. They have the same challenges and concerns as anyone else and are as susceptible to bad days as you or I.

Being an independent rep for multiple companies in today's health care climate can best be described at times as a treat. The pressures from many sources can be overwhelming and sometimes the person in the field gets blamed for lack of results when patience is one of the most important tools we have at our disposal.

The corporate world is no different. There are many hats that depend on your efforts all of which are important and essential. And you depend on theirs. Internalizing the team concept is a critical element to everyone's success and it's your job to lead that effort if no one else does.

My primary strategy in that pursuit, as I've mentioned before, is to keep everyone informed all the time. That would involve sales managers, customer service, other peers in the field and anyone else who's part of the overall effort. Even if the results aren't yet in the system they'll see that it's only a matter of time and that you're doing everything the right way.

It can be tough to be patient when everyone's at the home office staring at the phone that's not ringing. Frustration mounts and they take it out on you.

One of the companies that I represent offers a great device that's expensive with a long sales cycle. The head of customer service for some reason thought she was a sales manager one day and came at me with guns ablaze doing everything possible to unmotivate me. In that case, since I had zero time for nonsense, I got slightly angry and gave an accurate assessment of the real world.

That may have been a little harsh, but she periodically brings it up and we all laugh. Working hard and being outstanding gives you the right to tell it like it is. Sometimes we hold back out of fear of pressing the wrong buttons, but if someone's out of control and can't handle the truth then it's on them and not on you. And chances are that they'll get it and calm down.

It's not a perfect world, but is made much more so when we exude a sincere desire to do our best and work well with others.

Our customers, too, have very bad days and to say that they might take it out on you is the understatement of the millennia. A little understanding and compassion go a long way. Even those customers who actually are terrible people are probably those most in need of a periodic supporting shoulder so never take their behavior personally. Just be the kind and pleasant person you always are and everyone wins.

I Just Knew It

I try to not sweat the small stuff. As a matter of fact I also resist sweating the big stuff. There's a quality of optimism that I just know that everything will work out no matter what.

I actually get a lot of flak about that. It might seem a bit lackadaisical, but optimism is often misunderstood. There were even a handful of incidents as a Marine Corps Officer where it may have been expected of me to be a little more uptight than I was, but when push came to shove I'm the guy you wanted by your side.

Not to sound like a cliché, but I would honestly laugh during really tough times to the point of it probably being inappropriate, but I delivered every time. Now that you mention it I reflect back to other Marines who's sense of humor seemed to be in direct correlation to their competence and some who were very serious who may have fallen a bit short from an inability to fully connect with others.

When you put in the effort, persist and evolve you just know that you're on the right track; even if you're the only one. No one else has to believe in you except for you.

Many are very much on the right track, but deflated by others for one reason or another. Sometimes it's a well-meaning family member, a sales manager in desperate need of your leadership or a peer that isn't looking long-term as they try to (unsuccessfully) undermine your efforts. People can be wacky, but that's OK. They've always been that way, the supply is endless and it's not changing.

My mom used to say that water seeks its own level meaning that you tend to become like those you hang out with. Try to surround yourself with other positive thinkers like yourself.

I really come from a very unremarkable background, but almost as far back as I can remember I just knew that I'd be able to achieve anything that I set my mind to. We all have that capacity, but it gets suppressed from time to time.

Getting back to "Freedom, Opportunity and Apathy" - we are a product of our decisions and experiences so there's no point in being held hostage by negative people. The only thing that you can count on is change with discouragement and failure proof positive that you're on your way to untold success in any chosen endeavor.

Your thoughts over time are what get programed into your subconscious to guide your behavior. And if you do nothing wrong then you obviously are doing nothing and a welcome member of the 98% Club.

I look back at all of my experiences and failures and it's clear as day that nothing ever went wrong. It's all been a perfect path to a very exceptional today.

The Faith Multiplier

Something strange happens when you believe in yourself. It just keeps building and building and building.

The same can be said about negative thinking - it just keeps building and building and building.

Faith is often religious in nature with the spiritual effect being very real. I personally think it's a little conceited to think that we're fully in charge. There's just too much evidence of a higher being that gives us all of the tools we'll ever need.

One of those tools is free-will. We can choose whatever path we like and they're all available to us regardless of background.

The world-class athlete doesn't first become world-class and then start thinking like a world-class athlete. They begin their journey to superstardom by thinking world-class thoughts, which become world-class behaviors and then world-class results.

The formula is simple. We often look at those who have achieved the highest levels of success and can't comprehend ourselves in that position. Well, you're wrong and those you admire are no different than you. Very little separates first place from last.

So you might as well reject the forces of evil wherever they may lay, believe in your ability even if you have to temporarily fake it and put in the effort that others before you have expended to get to where you'd like to be.

The Faith Multiplier is exponential so you know what to do and now's a great time to start if you haven't already.

I Still Know Nothing

I'm almost in my mid-50's with my wife constantly showing me brochures of over-55 communities. That doesn't even make sense. There's no way that I'm almost 55, but I guess I am. It does beat the alternative so there's that.

You'd think that I would, at this point, have all the answers. One of my peers is 10 years younger than I and just brilliant. You'd think that he would come to me for guidance, but the opposite is more often the case.

We work together with 2 product lines and he's the one tasked with managing the territory. Almost every time we interact I'm just amazed at his perception and skill in putting a strategy together.

I often take his advice and the results are often exceptional.

No matter how accomplished we are there's others with similar experience that we can really learn a lot from. One of his signature approaches when putting in enormous effort for an evaluation of a high-end expensive device is to establish the expectation up front of the sales cycle (partly that it doesn't drag on) and that the business will be asked for once the evaluation is complete.

I used to absolutely do whatever the customer asks of me no questions asked, but that can (and often does) lead to abuse, indecision and a lot of wasted time. It's important to accommodate, but equally important for customers to be respectful of your time, effort and skill.

Setting that stage of expectation is up to you and requires a fine balance that will define you as a professional. This is precisely why you will make the big bucks.

What really counts is what you learn after you know it all.

Moving the Needle

Even the shark with his small brain and constant motion always has a purpose. Imagine what he could achieve with a larger brain, let's say, the size of ours.

Every time we sit down to do paperwork, make phone calls or venture out to sell we must do so with a purpose. I remember one day when living in Philadelphia during the big snow storm of the mid-1990's I couldn't get my car out so set out on foot to see how many cold calls I could complete.

I was unstoppable, persistent and driven with a single-minded focus as I approached 40+ cold calls. One prospect started asked questions and my first thought was, "I don't have time for this. I have more people to meet." That would be the opposite of moving-the-needle.

Another example was my first week in the corporate world spending that time in the field with an established rep before training started. He's really an awesome guy. We pulled up to a hospital and just sat there in the parking lot. I wasn't sure what was going on and he said, "We have an appointment here this morning, but I forget why."

It's easy to leave information at the front desk in the outside chance that we're actually accomplishing something when there's a good chance that we're not.

Try to have a plan, leave a personalized note on a brochure if you can't see anyone and, most importantly, try to get the appointment.

Have a goal in mind for the appointment. Have your brochures, etc. very well organized so that the focus is on your presentation and not on the disarray of brochures and other supporting materials that are all over the place.

Your overall strategy is designed to help the customer to achieve their goals. Your tool is leadership with the best interests of others as your guide. We all have a will to succeed, but much more important is the will to prepare to succeed. Set goals and set them high with their achievement determined by the quality of the journey.

Thanks again for taking the time and I'm available at my personal email address of corsteiner@aol.com if you have any questions, advice or input.

I hope you enjoyed "In Search of the Wholey Sale" and feel compelled to share it with others. Please let me know, either way, if you get a chance so I can make the next volume even better.

www.ingramcontent.com/pod-product-compliance
Lightning Source LLC
Chambersburg PA
CBHW070102210526
45170CB00012B/706